It's My Body

Legs, Knees, Feet, and Toes

Lola M. Schaefer

Heinemann Library
Chicago, Illinois

Designed by Sue Emerson, Heinemann Library; Page layout by Que-Net Media
Printed and bound in the United States by Lake Book Manufacturing, Inc.
Photo research by Jennifer Gillis

07 06 05 04 03
10 9 8 7 6 5 4 3 2 1

Library of Congress Cataloging-in-Publication Data
Schaefer, Lola M., 1950-
    Legs, knees, feet, and toes / Lola M. Schaefer.
        v. cm. – (It's my body)
Includes index.
Contents: What are your legs and feet? – Where are your legs? – What do your legs look like? – What's inside your legs? – What can you do with your legs? – Where are your feet? – What do your feet look like? – What's inside your feet? – What can you do with your feet? – Quiz – Picture glossary.
    ISBN 1-4034-0890-4 (HC), 1-4034-3482-4 (Pbk.)
    1. Leg–Juvenile literature. [1. Leg. 2. Foot. 3. Human anatomy.] I.Title. II.Series.
    QM549 .S37 2003
    612'.98–dc21

2002014739

Acknowledgments
The author and publishers are grateful to the following for permission to reproduce copyright material:
pp. 4, 8, 14 Robert Lifson/Heinemann Library; p. 5 Vic Thomasson/Rex Intstock/Stock Connection/PictureQuest; pp. 6, 15, 22, 24 Brian Warling/Heinemann Library; p. 7 Ginny Nichols/Stock Connection/PictureQuest; p. 9 Chris Carroll/Corbis; p. 10 Custom Medical Stock Photo; p. 12 Bob Daemmrich/Stock Boston Inc./PictureQuest; p. 13 Kari Weatherly/Corbis; p. 16 Charles O'Rear/Cobis; p. 17 Ted Horowitz/Corbis Stock Market; p. 18 Collection CNRI/PhotoTake; p. 19 DigitalVision/PictureQuest; p. 20 Geroge Shelley/Corbis; p. 21 Paul Barton/Corbis; p. 23 row 1 (L-R) Brian Warling/Heinemann Library, Ginny Nichols/Stock Connection/PictureQuest; row 2 Custom Medical Stock Photo; row 3 (L-R) George Shelley/Corbis, Brian Warling/Heinemann Library; back cover Brian Warling/Heinemann Library

Cover photograph by Larry Williams/Corbis

Every effort has been made to contact copyright holders of any material reproduced in this book. Any omissions will be rectified in subsequent printings if notice is given to the publisher.

Special thanks to our advisory panel for their help in the preparation of this book:

Alice Bethke, Library Consultant
Palo Alto, CA

Eileen Day, Preschool Teacher
Chicago, IL

Kathleen Gilbert,
Second Grade Teacher
Round Rock, TX

Sandra Gilbert,
Library Media Specialist
Fiest Elementary School
Houston, TX

Jan Gobeille,
Kindergarten Teacher
Garfield Elementary
Oakland, CA

Angela Leeper,
Educational Consultant
North Carolina Department
of Public Instruction
Wake Forest, NC

Some words are shown in bold, **like this.**
You can find them in the picture glossary on page 23.

Contents

What Are Your Legs and Feet?

Legs and feet are parts of your body.

Your body is made up of many parts.

Each part of your body does a job.

Your legs and feet help you stand, walk, and play.

Where Are Your Legs?

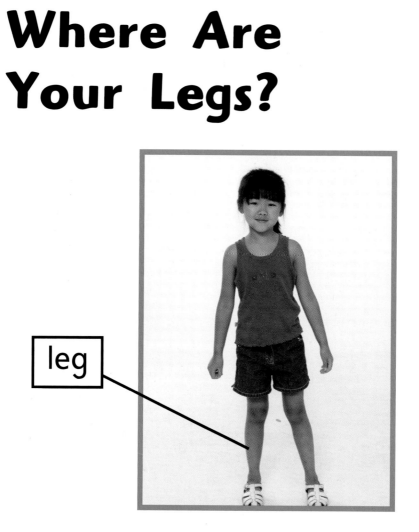

leg

Your legs are under your body.

They hold up your body.

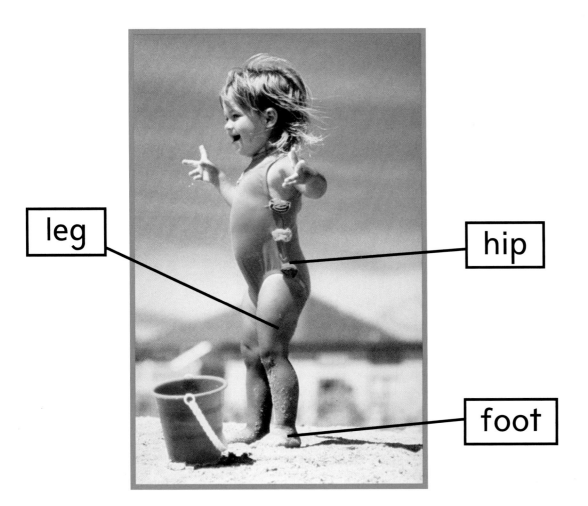

leg

hip

foot

Legs join your body at your **hips.**

Legs are between your hips
and feet.

What Do Your Legs Look Like?

Legs look like **tubes.**

They are a little wider at the top.

Smooth skin covers your legs.

Legs can bend to look like
the letter V.

What Is Inside Your Legs?

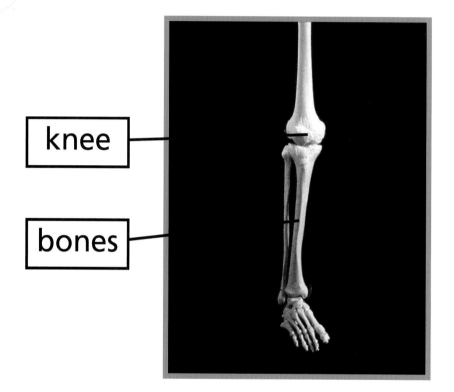

knee

bones

Bones are inside your legs.

Your leg bones meet at your **knee.**

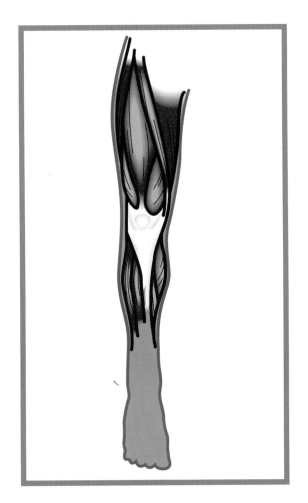

Muscles are inside your legs.

Muscles help your **bones** move.

What Can You Do with Your Legs?

You can stand on your legs.

Your legs help you dance.

Your legs help you run and jump.

They can help you ride a bike.

Where Are Your Feet?

Feet are at the ends of your legs.

Ankles join your feet to your legs.

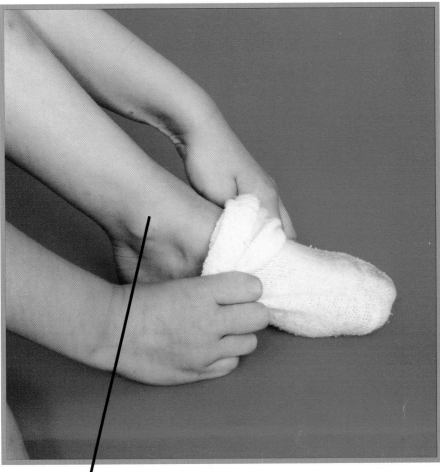

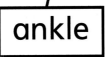

ankle

Ankles are **joints** that help your feet move.

What Do Your Feet Look Like?

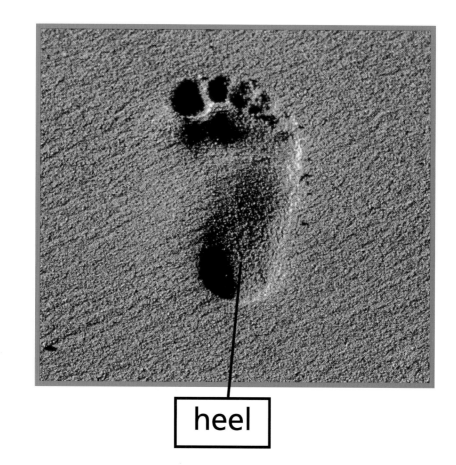

heel

Your feet are shaped like **ovals**.

You have round **heels** on the backs of your feet.

You have five toes on each foot.

Each toe is a different size.

What Is Inside Your Feet?

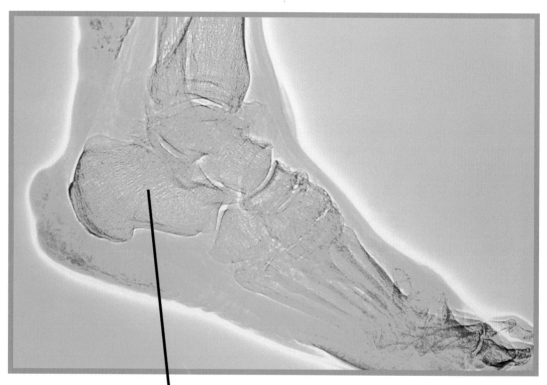

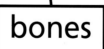

bones

Bones are inside your feet.

Bones fit together at **joints**.

Muscles are inside your feet.

Muscles help move the bones in your feet.

What Can You Do with Your Feet?

Your feet help you stand.

You kick with your feet when you swim.

Your feet can grip what is
beneath them.

You can kick a ball with
your feet.

Quiz

Can you guess what these are?

Look for the answers on page 24.

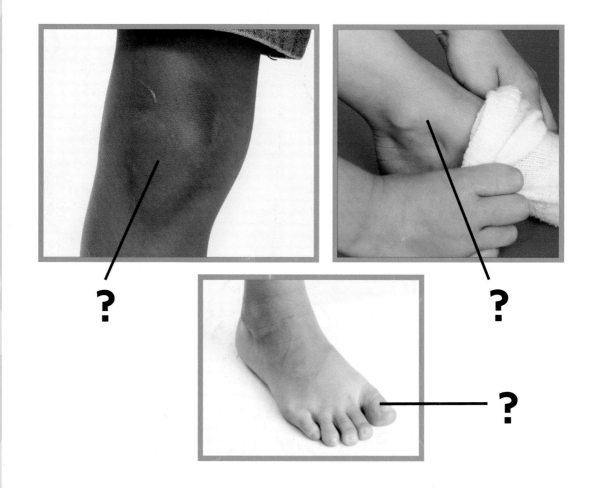

?

?

?

Picture Glossary

ankle
pages 14, 15

hip
page 7

muscle
pages 11, 19

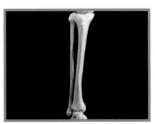

bone
pages 10, 11,
18, 19

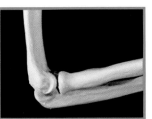

joint
pages 15, 18

oval
page 16

heel
page 16

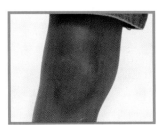

knee
page 10

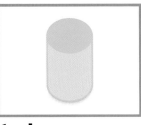

tube
page 8

23

Note to Parents and Teachers

Reading for information is an important part of a child's literacy development. Learning begins with a question about something. Help children think of themselves as investigators and researchers by encouraging their questions about the world around them. Each chapter in this book begins with a question. Read the question together. Look at the pictures. Talk about what you think the answer might be. Then read the text to find out if your predictions were correct. Think of other questions you could ask about the topic, and discuss where you might find the answers. Assist children in using the picture glossary and the index to practice new vocabulary and research skills.

Index

Answers to quiz on page 22

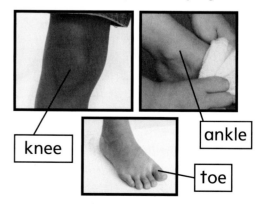

knee

ankle

toe

24